CLB 1947
© 1987 Illustrations and text: Colour Library Books Ltd,
    Guildford, Surrey, England.
Printed and bound in Barcelona, Spain by Cronion, S.A.
All rights reserved.
1987 edition published by Crescent Books, distributed by Crown Publishers, Inc.
ISBN 0 517 639513
h g f e d c b a

HAWAII

Text by

Bill Harris

Designed and Produced by

Ted Smart & David Gibbon

CRESCENT BOOKS
NEW YORK

IN the style of architecture that builders of shopping centers and suburban housing call "Early American," a decoration in the form of a pineapple often appears over doorways and on fence posts. The symbolism of the pineapple goes back to the old whalers who took long voyages out of New England. When they returned home, they usually had a lot more on board than the products of whales they had found. They had exotic treasure from the South Seas and they had stories to tell as well. Naturally, their neighbors were interested, and so, as a sign that the Captain was home and receiving visitors, a fresh pineapple was placed outside his front door. Eventually, as often happens, people began carving the pineapples from wood or from stone as a more permanent sign of hospitality.

The pineapple is also one of the symbols of Hawaii; and that's entirely appropriate because so is hospitality.

James Michener has said that Hawaii's real flowers are its people. He said there are more conspicuously beautiful young women in Hawaii than anywhere else in the United States, and added that the young men are just as handsome. Anyone who's ever been there will agree with that, and probably vouch for the fact that they are among the warmest, most hospitable people on earth.

It hasn't always been exactly like that. When Captain James Cook, the first European to discover Hawaii, landed there in 1778, he was "pleasantly surprised" by the welcoming party that rowed out into the harbor to meet his ship. But the pleasure faded when the first shore party found that the natives were dedicated thieves. They weren't too subtle about it, either. They took oars, muskets, anything at all that wasn't tied down. And they wouldn't stop until one of them was shot by a sailor. With that shot, civilization officially arrived in the place Cook named the "Sandwich Islands."

The Polynesians Cook found there were of the same race he had found in far-off Tahiti. "How shall we account for this nation spreading itself over this vast ocean?" he wrote. And until this day, no one has been able to account for it. They thought Cook was their long-lost White god Lono, and when he went ashore for the first time, something happened that he had never seen before, even though he had been to, even discovered, some of the most exotic places in all the world. "The very instant I leaped ashore, they all fell flat on their faces," he recorded. A year later these same people killed Cook when he turned his back on them.

None of that is to say that Cook and others who followed him found all the native Hawaiians to be thieving, hostile savages. But they were a primitive people, and life for them was less than easy. Human sacrifices were common, the chiefs of the different islands kept them in an almost constant state of bloody war, and their chiefs were generally cruel men. In spite of it all, they were handsome and beautiful, childlike and trusting.

Mark Twain, who toured the Islands on horseback in the mid-19th century, explains what they were like and how they changed: "Human sacrifices were offered up in those old bygone days when the simple child of nature, yielding momentarily to sin when sorely tempted, acknowledged his error when calm reflection had shown it to him, and came forward with noble frankness and offered up his grandmother as an atoning sacrifice – in those old days when the luckless sinner could keep on cleansing his conscience and achieving periodical happiness as long as his relations held out; long, long before the missionaries braved a thousand privations to come and make them permanently miserable by telling them how beautiful and how blissful a place heaven is, and how nearly impossible it is to get there; and showed the poor native how dreary a place perdition is and what unnecessarily liberal facilities there are for going to it; showed him how, in his ignorance, he had gone and fooled away all his kinfolks to no purpose; showed him what rapture it is to work all day long for fifty cents to buy food for the next day with, as compared to fishing for a pastime and lolling in the shade through eternal summer, and eating the bounty that nobody labored to provide but Nature. How sad it is to think of the multitudes who went to their graves in this beautiful island and never knew there was a hell!"

"Paradise" is a word that's used more often than any other to describe the Hawaiian Islands. That's because no other word fits quite so well. It's not uncommon to hear tourists remark that if heaven isn't like this, they don't want to go there. And tourists are going to Hawaii in waves as spectacular as the seaborne waves that break on those fabulous beaches. About three-million visitors arrive in Hawaii every year, mostly from the United States. But of the million-plus Japanese tourists who visit the United States every year, 75 percent go to Hawaii. Japanese-Americans rank second in numbers behind "Haole," the name native Hawaiians use for mainland whites, so visitors from Japan feel right at home. Just as important, probably, is the fact that Honolulu is just six jet hours from Tokyo.

The jet plane is what's behind the Hawaiian tourist boom. Back in the 1950s, when Hawaii became a state, most Americans who went there were from California, and most of them went by boat. It was a leisurely, unforgettable experience for them. One man, who made the trip several times, describes it this way:

"On the fourth morning out from San Francisco, you'd wake up to see Molokai there on the left and and Oahu on the right. Rounding Diamond Head, the biggest thing on the island looked to be a pink Moorish palace, the Royal Hawaiian Hotel.

"The ship would take on three tugloads of greeters, and move on to the dock at Aloha Tower, where the Royal Hawaiian Band and hula girls met you."

The weekly arrival of the big white ship "Lurline" from San Francisco was called "Steamer Day" in the Honolulu of the '50s. The mainlanders, who had invested five days to get there, got a welcome that was unrivalled anywhere in the world. The air was perfumed with the heavy scent of tropical flowers, the green mountains accented the dramatic cliffs and the beautiful white beaches presented a picture that could only conjure up that same word again, "paradise."

And to add pleasure to the paradise, the mainlanders

were met by those beautiful hula girls singing the love songs of their Polynesian ancestors, while in the water below the slowly moving ship, native divers raced to the bottom of the crystal clear harbor to retrieve silver dollars tossed overboard by the visitors. It put everyone in the mood for a party, and it wasn't uncommon for the party to last until the following day when the famous Hawaiian sun lured everyone down to the beach.

People who go to Hawaii today get there faster and spend less time getting acclimated when they do. But the legendary hospitality that is Hawaii and the spectacular beauty make their first impression of the place just as memorable today as it ever was.

The Islands, flung like a strand of pearls into the middle of the Pacific Ocean, are about 2,500 miles from San Francisco. There are about 132 islands in all, some not inhabited at all, some the private preserves of single families. In total area, Hawaii is two-thirds the size of Sicily, but bigger than Massachusetts. The eight major islands in the Southeast: Hawaii, Oahu, Maui, Kahoolawe, Kauai, Molokai and Niihau, make up all but three square miles of the total area. And of the major islands, one isn't inhabited at all. Kahoolawe is used by the military as a target island for bombing and artillery practice.

Honolulu and Pearl Harbor are on the island of Oahu, which is where some 80 percent of the state's population lives. The biggest island, Hawaii, is also the farthest south and, in fact, is the Southernmost point in the United States, at the tip of Volcanoes National Park.

It's always spring in Hawaii because of the cooling winds from the Pacific, which keep the year round temperature in the neighborhood of 75°F. And the sun is shining just about all the time. The Islanders thank one of their gods, Maui, for that. They say that many years ago he hid in the forest until the sun came out. When it did, he lassoed it and tied it down so it couldn't move. The sun didn't like that very much, according to the legend, but Maui wouldn't let it go until it promised to move more slowly across his islands. A promise given is a promise kept when you're the sun. And the promise is still being kept all these centuries later.

If you were playing a word association game and someone said "Hawaii," it wouldn't be long before someone else said "Hula." Hawaii didn't have a written language before the missionaries came in the 19th century, and the tradition of the people was handed down through the movement of the hands in this graceful dance, much in the same way Africans kept the past alive with an oral tradition. In the very early days, the dance was done only by men. Women got into the act generations ago, of course, and that's another nice thing about Hawaii.

Hula schools in Hawaii are as popular as ballet schools in the rest of the country, and today boys as well as girls are learning it. It takes all forms, from a slow and sensual dance to the bump and grind associated with carnivals and waterfront bars. An agent in Honolulu, who provides dancers for weddings and bar mitzvahs, says, "the hula can be sexy as hell, but it should also be innocent as hell."

"All the dancers I've ever worked with," she says, "are extremely modest girls who would squeal like hell if a man walked into their dressing room while they were in their bra and panties. But they think nothing of performing before an audience and shaking their hips in a Tahiti skirt cut several inches below the navel."

Another agent who was asked to provide a topless hula dancer found that none of the regular island dancers would do it. He solved the problem by going to the mainland for a dark-skinned girl who would.

What makes the hula something special is the complete innocence the dancers project, all the while moving their bodies in a decidedly sexual way. It isn't easy of course, and those girls from the mainland, dark-skinned or not, just can't duplicate it.

The legend of how the hula began, undoubtedly handed down in the language of dance, is that the sister of the fire goddess, Pele, was such a wonderful dancer that she mesmerized her sister into following her to the caves in the northern part of Oahu. Because of the wonder of it all, Pele is presumably still there.

Hula was a national institution when the missionaries arrived. An institution they didn't much care for! The shocked Christians from New England immediately set out to dress the hula girls in high-collared, long-sleeved blouses and long skirts. That took most of the fun out of it, and the dance died out rather quickly! In 1883, King Kalakaua brought it back as part of the ceremonies at his coronation. They danced 252 different kinds of hula for him! Which goes to show that you can't keep a good idea down forever!

Leis are as Hawaiian as the hula, and they're usually used as a sign of welcome or farewell. In the early days they were reserved for royalty, and they were always made from feathers. Today most are made of flowers, although in some quarters plastic seems to be considered fashionable. Sometimes they're made of white and yellow ginger blossoms that smell as beautiful as they look. Frangipani is another common lei flower. Its overlapping petals add a special beauty to the garland, and the aroma lets you know you're in the tropics. Carnations and orchids also make beautiful leis and add to the wide variety you can buy all over the islands from street vendors and flower shops.

If the hula and the lei are typically Hawaiian, so is the Polynesian language. But the language isn't exclusively Hawaiian. Indeed, when Captain Cook first landed there, he had no trouble talking with the natives, which pleased him no end because it made it possible for him to place a large order for provisions for his ship. Which, no doubt, pleased the natives no end! Cook had learned the language in Tahiti, where, incidentally, the crew of one of his ships was killed and eaten for dinner by the natives.

Hawaii is the only state with its own language, and some of its words like "lanai," which means "porch," and "muumuu," a loose-fitting, nonrevealing dress mandated by the missionaries, have become part of the basic language of the mainland. Every word in the Hawaiian language ends in a vowel. Consonants are never used without a vowel between them, but whole strings of vowels can come together. There's a basic rule that *a, e, i, o* and *u* are pronounced separately, but sometimes combinations like *au*, which gets pronounced like the *ow* in "cow," offer enough exceptions to keep you on your toes. The fact is, vowels are the mainstay of the Hawaiian language because they have only seven consonants to choose from. The ones they recognize are *h, k, m, n, p,* and *w*.

It all adds up to a very melodious-sounding language. Even the word for "anger," "huhu," makes you happy when you hear it. If a Hawaiian wants you to get a move on, the word for it is "wikiwiki." If that doesn't work, you'll probably be in "pilikia," "trouble."

The work "Kamaaina" is usually used to describe a native-born Hawaiian descended from the native chiefs or the missionaries. They have traditionally run the businesses of Hawaii, and figure prominently in the social structure of the Islands. In the early days, native chiefs kept their position (and their heads) at the whim of the king. And the person of the king changed as frequently as the whim, so the land changed hands on a fairly regular basis. Descendants of the missionaries overthrew the traditional Hawaiian monarchy and introduced Western ideas about who owned what. King Kamehameha II went along with the new idea and convinced some 240 chiefs they should, too. Their descendants are the "Kamaaina" of today.

But who were those missionaries who took the word of paradise to paradise itself? There were ten groups of them, Calvinists all, who were sent out from Boston by the American Board of Commissioners for Foreign Missions to give the gift of Christianity to the heathen. They arrived in the early 19th century, 184-strong. Many of them died, more went home to New England. But 52 families, the strongest of the lot, stayed on to produce more than 5,000 descendants. And to change the course of Hawaiian history.

They didn't like what they found there. "Public nakedness and lewd dancing" were first on the agenda of things to be done away with, and they saw their job clearly: it wouldn't be enough to save sinners, they would have to civilize these savages at the same time.

It wasn't easy for the missionaries at first, but as Yankee Calvinists, "easy" didn't matter much to them. Slowly they befriended the chiefs and members of the royal family, but they were never able to touch the soul of King Liholiho. Then one day, Liholiho decided to travel to London for a chat with his "friend," King George IV.

He wasn't gone long before the people of Hawaii were told not to do a thing, including lighting a fire, on the Sabbath. Before much longer, the chiefs and head men were ordered to make sure their people obeyed the new rule and, furthermore, attended both the church and the mission school. One chief refused and, unfortunately for him, his father died leaving all his land to the king. In retaliation for this affront, he decided to go to war with the Government. And lost the battle.

The volunteers who defeated him had prayed to the Christian God, had refused to do battle on the Sabbath, and

refrained from killing the rebel when it was all over. All this, plus the fact that they had done it without the leadership of the king, made them begin to take the ways of this new god a little more seriously.

Meanwhile the king and the queen both died in London of measles, a common disease in Britain, but quite alien to this pair of "damned cannibals," as King George was heard to call them. They were returned home and buried with great ceremony by the Christians, even though the king had never accepted their church himself. This further impressed the chiefs, who were now eager to accept the teachings of the missionaries, and their people eagerly followed them.

The Missionaries weren't the only white people on the Islands in the 1800s. There were hunters and sailors and others who had little truck with these upright folk from Boston. The missionaries paid little attention to them, either, at first. But they began to notice the missionaries when the newly Christianized chiefs began suppressing such things as drunkenness and debauchery, and, most important, the renting of women. At one point, a boatload of sailors actually attacked the home of one of the missionaries, who escaped with his life only because the Christian chiefs came to his rescue.

The U.S. Navy even intervened, telling the chiefs it wasn't unusual for civilized countries to allow prostitution. But Christian truth and Yankee perseverance won the day.

By the 1830s, the missionaries found that most of their troubles were behind them, and they were joined by a new breed of evangelists from New England whose brand of preaching "broke sinners down," and brought them to repentance with "the battle-axe of the Lord." In a single day in 1838, no less than 1,705 converts were baptized into what may have been the biggest Protestant congregation anywhere in the world.

It was only a matter of time before they became powerful in politics, too, and they used their influence to get American support for a Hawaii free from the influences of other foreign countries, especially Britain and France.

Then they began to buy the place.

In 1835, three young men from New England arrived in Honolulu. One of them had been a student at Yale Theological Seminary, but they didn't come to save souls. Their game, as it turned out, was real estate.

Within a few years, they made a secret agreement with the king that gave them exclusive rights to all unoccupied and undeveloped land in the islands. Then they set out to peddle those rights in the United States and Europe. Apparently, their timing was wrong because they couldn't find any interested buyers anywhere except in Belgium, and even that prospect finally died. Eventually, their agent returned to Hawaii with a ticket he had no money to pay for.

The bankruptcy trials that followed were nasty and drove a wedge between the Western businessmen and the missionaries. But through it all, the missionaries became convinced that land reform was essential and their role in it indispensable.

Under Hawaiian tradition, the common people had no

rights in the land. The chiefs knew that land was power because it was the source of life. As one missionary wrote: "from uka, mountain, whence came wood, kapa, for clothing, olona, for fish line, ti-leaf for wrapping paper, ie for rattan lashing, wild birds for food, to the sea, kai, whence came ia, fish, and all connected therewith," all the necessities of life were easily available to everyone.

The missionaries felt that industry and thrift were important virtues, and the only way to encourage those virtues in the common people was to allow them to become land owners. There were winds of change all over the world at that time and the chiefs knew they had to face the fact that it would come to them as well. They were slow to accept the idea though, and it wasn't until 1846 that commoners were allowed to buy their own land. The land division was called the Great Mahele. It allowed the king to retain vast estates for himself and for the chiefs to buy title to the land they already held. The big breakthrough was for the commoners, who were now allowed to buy tiny lots, called *kuleanas,* for themselves.

Foreigners weren't allowed to share in the Great Mahele, but could lease land for a period of 50 years. The Hawaiian people, meanwhile, bought their kuleanas by billing the government for services they had performed free for the king. The king's tailor, for instance, was given a lot in Nuuanu Valley. The man who piloted the king's ship got a town lot in Honolulu and about four acres in Waikiki!

It wasn't long, of course, before the law was changed to allow foreigners into the act. And that was the beginning of the end as far as the natives were concerned. The idea of the independent family farm never caught on with the Hawaiians. Taro was the main crop, and growing it was hard work. Now that they were free of their chiefs, they used the freedom to move away from them. They knew that the freedom to buy land also gave them the freedom to sell it, and that was the option they chose.

And guess who bought it from them? By the end of the 19th century, the white men owned four acres to every one acre of land owned by the native Hawaiians and their chiefs.

Property values in Hawaii today are incredible by any standard, and the cost of housing is going up at a rate of some 20 percent a year. On the Island of Maui, recently, condominiums in a fashionable town were selling for $270,000. Two years before, the same apartments cost $90,000. Hawaii's land fever is converting huge tracts of undeveloped land, some of it on the sides of still-active volcanoes, into new towns and resorts at a pace that would have amazed the easy-going Polynesians who were there before the white man came. The prices would have amazed the white men themselves. If you can find a vacation cottage for less than $50,000, buy it. It's a comparative steal.

Mainlanders, some of whom have never set foot on the Islands, are buying building lots sight unseen for $2,000 an acre and more. The name of the game is speculation, even though much of the land is virtually useless because there is no water, nor any prospect of getting it there. Other investors find Hawaii n condominiums the answer to a

dream. They buy a share in a development, which legall stays undivided and in the hands of an association set up t take care of the grounds and to generate more income b renting the units to vacationers. When the condominiu owner goes to Hawaii for a meeting of the association, h deducts the cost of the trip from his income tax as a busine expense!

It's a proposition that's hard to turn down, and it become a challenge to the Hawaiian government. The co of housing has gone well beyond the reach of man Hawaiians, and some have moved into run-down shant towns that have none of the charm of the little grass shack of their ancestors. But, like their ancestors, they hav discovered that the best thing about being able to buy land that you can also sell it. Almost any property owner ther will tell you the government's effort to put limits o expansion is an idea whose time has come. But every ne development scheme, and there are plenty of them, is a opportunity that puts a strain on the limits, and it's easy t say, "let's allow this one because it will bring new jobs for th people."

When Mark Twain arrived in Honolulu more than 10 years ago, he wrote: "The more I traveled through the tow the better I liked it. Every step revealed a new contrast…I place of the grand mud-colored brown fronts of Sa Francisco, I saw dwellings of straw, adobes and crean colored pebble-and-shell conglomerated coral…also a grea number of neat white cottages, with green window shutter In place of front yards like billiard tables with iron fenc around them, I saw these homes surrounded by ample yard thickly clad with green grass and shaded by tall trees.…I place of the customary geranium, calla lily, etc., languishin in dust and general debility, I saw luxurious banks an thickets of flowers, fresh as a meadow after a rain, an glowing with the richest dyes. In place of San Francisc pleasure grove, the 'Willows,' I saw huge-bodied, wid spreading forest trees with strange names and strang appearance – trees that cast a shadow like a thundercloud ar were able to stand alone without being tied to green poles.

"…I looked on a multitude of people, some white, i white coats, vests, pantaloons, even white cloth shoes, mac snowy with chalk duly laid on every morning; but th majority of people were almost as dark as Negroes – wome with comely features, fine black eyes, rounded form inclining to the voluptuous, clad in a single bright red c white garment that fell free and unconfined from should to heel, long black hair falling loose, gypsy hats, encircl with wreaths of natural flowers of a brilliant carmine tir plenty of dark men in various costumes, and some wit nothing on but a battered stovepipe hat tilted on the nos and a very scant breechclout. Certain children were cloth in nothing but sunshine – a very neat-fitting and picturesqu apparel indeed.

"Instead of roughs and rowdies staring and blackguardir on the corners, I saw long-haired, saddle-colored Sandwic Island maidens sitting on the ground in the shade of corn houses.…Instead of wretched cobblestone pavements, walked on a firm foundation of coral, built up from the bottom of the sea by the absurd but persevering insect of that name, with a light layer of lava and cinders overlying (it).

"Instead of cramped and crowded streetcars, I met dusky native women sweeping by, free as the wind on fleet horses with gaudy riding sashes streaming like banners behind them.

"Instead of the combined stenches of Chinadom and Brannon Street slaughterhouses, I breathed the balmy fragrance of jessamine, oleander and the pride of India. In place of the hurry and bustle and noisy confusion of San Francisco, I moved in the midst of a summer calm as tranquil as dawn in the Garden of Eden. In place of the Golden City's skirting sand hills and the placid bay, I saw on one side a framework of tall, precipitous mountains close at hand, clad in refreshing green and cleft by deep, cool, chasmlike valleys. In front, the grand sweep of the ocean: a brilliant, transparent green near the shore, bound and bordered by a long white line of foamy spray dashing against the reef. Farther out, the dead water of the deep sea, flecked with whitecaps. In the far horizon, a single, lonely sail – a mere accent mark to emphasize a slumberous calm and solitude that were without sound or limit. When the sun sunk down – the one intruder from other realms and persistent in suggestions of them – it was tranced luxury to sit in the perfumed air and forget that there was any world but these enchanted islands."

Mark Twain wouldn't recognize Honolulu today. But then, he wouldn't recognize San Francisco, either. The neat little buildings he saw have been replaced by something quite different, and today's traveler's first impression of the place is usually the long row of high-rise buildings on Waikiki Beach. The city has now become a place of skyscrapers and souvenir shops, tour buses and the biggest resort hotels in the world. It's a bustling city with an ethnic mix that makes it different from almost any other city in the United States.

Honolulu is the capital city and its population reflects the mixture of people you'll find in all the islands. Less than half are haoles, Western whites; about a quarter are Japanese and about 15 per cent are descended from the original Polynesians who were the first to arrive there. The balance of the population is Filipino, Chinese, Korean, Black and others.

It's an exotic blend that's sheer joy for people-watchers. The delicate features of the Japanese, the handsome faces of the Chinese, the legendary beauty of the Polynesians add up to a spectacle that's hard to resist. Even the haole seem more beautiful here than anywhere else.

Downtown Honolulu today isn't much different from Houston or any other American city that has gone through a building boom in the last twenty years. But don't let that fool you. There is a difference! Sure, Kalakaua Avenue, like main streets in other parts of the country, has been converted to a car-less shopping mall. The convention halls and continental restaurants are air-conditioned. And you stand a good chance of meeting someone from your home town when you go there on a vacation.

You begin to notice the difference when you sit on a terrace overlooking the Pacific and you're served local pineapple or papaya for breakfast. You see it in the side streets, or in a Chinese cemetery where families feed their dead to keep them contented. You hear it in the streets where the old Hawaiian songs still haunt the air. You get a sense of the past in Honolulu's Bishop Museum, founded as a memorial to a Hawaiian princess who married a New Englander at 18. Mrs Bishop was heiress to the lands and treasures of the Kamehameha family, and the treasures form the nucleus of the museum's collection. The old royal thrones and crowns are here, along with a rare collection of feathered adornment made for the chiefs and kings of old Hawaii. The rich colors and design of the cloaks impressed Captain Cook, who noted in his journal that "…even in countries where dress is more attended to, (they) might be reckoned elegant. The ground of them is a net-work upon which the most beautiful red and yellow feathers are so closely fixed that the surface might be compared to the thickest and richest velvet."

The Bishop Museum also has a planetarium, reflecting an interest in the stars that goes back to the earliest times. Today, one of the world's most important astronomical observatories is on the Island of Hawaii, at the top of Mount Mauna Kea. The summit of the volcano is almost 14,000 feet high, so high that clouds rarely pass over it, and astronomers feel it is the best place in the Northern Hemisphere for looking out into the universe.

The Island of Oahu, where Honolulu is located, is relatively small, and can be explored easily. It's ringed by beaches, the most famous of which is Waikiki. The Hawaiian royalty reserved Waikiki for themselves, but the Hawaiians of today have generally turned it over to the tourists. They go to Ala Moana Beach, not far away, for swimming and tanning. When it's surfing they want, they load their surfboards on their cars and head north to Makaha or another of the "big surf" beaches across the island. For snorkeling, they go to the underwater sanctuary at Hanauma Bay. For privacy, they pass the "Blowhole," a dramatic geyser that erupts every time the waves hit a hole in the lava ledge, sending a huge waterspout into the air, to get to Halona Cove, a small beach hidden away between the cliffs.

Diamond Head, an extinct volcano, is also on the Island of Oahu. You can go inside the crater and have a look around, if you like. The old Hawaiians called it Leahi, which means "the place of fire." It got a new name from British sailors who thought they had found diamonds there. What they really found were volcanic crystals.

Visitors to Oahu can get a glimpse of Samoa and Tahiti, New Zealand or Fiji by visiting the Polynesian Cultural Center. It's a collection of villages of the kind that would be found on the other islands with a Polynesian tradition. Young Polynesians work their way through college by demonstrating the old ways of life, singing and dancing in authentic native costume. Old Hawaii is there, too, in a village of triangular houses covered in pili grass…the famous "little grass shacks" you often hear about, but don't see much in Hawaii these days.

There's a bird sanctuary on Oahu, too. It's called Paradise Park (there's that word again!). There are also 15 golf courses, 90 tennis courts, 50 miles of beaches and 600 places to go surfing. And just so you don't get homesick, it has Ala Moana Shopping Center, one of the biggest in the world. Most of the hotels have their own shopping malls, too. In fact, about the only thing that makes the hotels of Oahu different from those you'd find in any American city with palm trees and a beach is that every one of them offers church services every Sunday morning in their schedule of activities. It's just one more way the influence of the missionaries hangs on.

Pearl Harbor, named for the pearl oysters that once thrived there, is part of the Oahu scene. The Hawaiians believed this was originally the home of Kaahupahua, the queen of the sharks. She lived, they said, in a cavern that was a majestic palace guarded by a brother shark. She protected the people by decreeing that sharks should not molest humans, and she backed her decree with an order to her shark people to be constantly on the alert to kill any man-eaters that might invade the waters near the island.

When the U.S. Navy began dredging the channel to open Pearl Harbor in 1900, they were warned by the Hawaiians that they were risking the wrath of both the gods and the sharks. To avoid it, they carefully removed a shrine that had been built in their path and took it, stone-by-stone, out to sea, where it was lowered carefully to the ocean floor in a reverent ceremony.

The jumbo jets deliver tourists hundreds at a time to Honolulu airport. If they're from New York, they've been on the plane for 13 hours and they've had to push their watches ahead another six hours. Or, if they prefer to be on the real Hawaiian time, they take their watches off. Radio and television stations are about the only institutions in the Islands that follow anything like a strict time schedule, and even they occasionally forget. There's a carillon in Waikiki that plays Hawaiian tunes as it strikes the hour, but the music rarely begins until the hour is at least 10 minutes old.

Most of the mainlanders and others who pass through the airport stay right on Oahu, but there is great enthusiasm building for the other islands. Many of them hop a hydrofoil to go 22 miles east to Molokai, the one they call "the friendly isle." Still a little off the beaten path, it manages to keep some of the character of the old Hawaii. For many years, it has been the site of a treatment center for leprosy. The colony at Kalaupapa was taken over by a Belgian priest, Father Joseph Damien de Veuster, in 1873. He found sub-human conditions there, and gave his life to building the settlement into a place of dignity and hope. The colony is still there, a memorial to Father Damien, the "Martyr of Molokai."

Molokai was slow to grow because water was scarce there. But it's plentiful in the mountains on the northern side, and the combination of lush forests and towering cliffs, some as high as 3,600 feet, make it the most majestically beautiful of all the islands. Fishing is great there, too. A shelf of land extends more than 25 miles out from the island,

making one of the richest fishing grounds in all of Hawaii. You'll find deer in the forests, too. They were put there in 1869 by the Duke of Edinburgh, who received them as a gift from the emperor of Japan. Apparently he didn't want to be bothered taking them back to England with him.

There are huge pineapple plantations on Molokai, and cattle ranches, too. King Kamehameha V himself raised longhorns out here in the 1860s. When he wasn't rasslin steers, he found time to plant a grove of 1,000 coconut trees on ten acres just outside Kaunakakai, the island's main town.

Just beyond Molokai is Lanai, the "Pineapple Island." It's owned by Castle & Cook, a company most people know because of a company it owns, the Dole Company. They bought this island, 18 by 13 miles wide, back in 1922 for $1,100,000. They built a company town there and transformed the island into a huge pineapple plantation with good roads, a deep-water port, camp grounds and a casual mountain hotel with fireplaces in the rooms.

Naturally, just about everybody on Lanai works for the pineapple company, but the shops, service stations, theater and such are all privately owned. The old natives say that Lanai was the home of evil spirits for 1,000 years after they arrived in the islands. An exile from Maui named Kaulalaau got rid of them and made it safe for human habitation, just like Saint Patrick did for Ireland. That was all many, many years ago, obviously, because archaeologists have found one of the best-preserved Hawaiian ruins in the islands at Kaunola, which was also a favorite fishing spot of Kamehameha the Great.

Lanai is also a paradise for hunters. It abounds in pronghorn antelope, partridge, pheasant and wild goats. In some parts of the island the season is open all the year for bow and arrow hunting.

Captain Vancouver, a British explorer who followed Captain Cook to the islands, described Lanai as a "naked island which seemed thinly covered with shriveled grass in a scorched state." He wouldn't recognize it today! Today hikers stroll through forests of Norfolk pine and the more than 13,000 acres of pineapple trees are in anything but a "scorched state."

For years, the "in" crowd, film stars and the like, have been going to the island of Maui, which is quite different from all the others. It was created by two big volcanoes that formed two mountain masses joined together by a thin strip of land. The strip of land is where you'll find most of the hotels and condominiums that make this the second most popular tourist island in Hawaii. One of the things they go there to see is Haleakala, the largest dormant volcano in the world. And it's worth the trip! The mountain is more than 10,000 feet high and the crater is 21 miles around. Inside it are caverns, a lake, meadows, forests, even a desert, and the biggest raspberry bushes you've ever seen.

Maui was a favorite stop for the whaling ships that passed by in the late 19th century. The seaport town of Lahaina was a lively place back then, with sailors fighting over the girls who swam out to meet their ships, or drawing knives and belaying pins just for the fun of it.

The whalers finally all went home, and sugar cane took over, which wasn't nearly as much fun for anybody. But it was quieter, and that made it attractive to tourists, which has now made Lahaina a lively town again. And the trip from the main town of Wailuku is breathtakingly beautiful. They've recreated the flavor of the old whaling town there, and though you're not likely to get hit on the head with a belaying pin, you'll find it a fascinating trip into the past. The annual Whaling Spree, a yacht race to Honolulu held in the fall, usually begins on the verandah of the Old Whaler's Grog Shop at the Pioneer Inn, a waterfront landmark, and possibly one of Maui's most popular spots. Just about five miles from it, the Kaanapali Coast is quickly becoming one of the most popular spots in all the islands. It has beautiful beaches on one side and majestic mountains on the other. But if that's not enough for pleasure-seeking travelers (and it rarely ever seems to be), the hand of man has added a couple of golf courses, a string of first-rate hotels and an airport that makes getting there simple. It even has a shopping center to keep the traveler from getting too homesick.

People who prefer natural beauty in its natural state find it on Kauai, probably the most relaxed of any of the islands. When people who make movies or television commercials are looking for an idyllic setting, they always wind up on Kauai.

The natives call it the "garden island," but its landscape includes some awesome cliffs and rugged canyons along with the brightly colored flowers and lush trees that spill over into the water at the edge of smooth sandy beaches. The beaches are nearly deserted most of the time, and inland you could spend hours wandering through quiet valleys and not see another soul.

Archaeologists have found remains of a culture that seems to have thrived on Kauai long before the Polynesians came. The Polynesians themselves have legends about it. They called them the "Menehune," and said they were a race of elflike creatures not more than three feet tall, capable of complex engineering feats like changing the course of rivers or damming them up to make better fishing holes. They worked only at night, of course, so not many people ever got to actually see them. But every once in a while somebody strolling in the moonlight near one of Kauai's spectacular waterfalls sees one of the little people hurrying by. Sightings are rare, but people who live there can show you plenty of examples of their work.

Photographers can't get enough of Kauai. Waimea Canyon is a place they adore because the look of the place changes from hour to hour as the light changes. The Wailua River, once considered so sacred it didn't have a name lest someone would be tempted to talk about it, is the scene of several ancient temples. One of them was called a "temple of refuge," placed there as a sanctuary where someone who had broken a tabu or had been defeated in battle could be guaranteed safety. But there was a catch: the transgressor had to get there ahead of the people who were chasing him.

One of Hawaii's most fascinating resort hotels, Coco Palms, is on Kauai. It was built to conform to the old traditions and to recreate as many of them as possible. Every evening at dusk, a group of young men sound a note on conch shells, first in the direction of the mountains, then toward the sea. It's an ancient signal to everyone within earshot that "the drums will talk." As they finish, the drums do talk in a beat that announces that a feast has been prepared. And that, in turn, signals the lighting of torches in the hotel's 30-acre palm grove.

The site of the hotel is the royal grove of the old Kauai kings, and the Coco Palms has a museum with mementos of the royalty who once played there.

There's a spectacular waterspout on this island, too. When the surf hits a hole in the rock called "Spouting Horn," it sends a jet of water 100 feet into the air. And when that happens, you can hear what sounds like a deep sigh from another hole nearby. It's the sound, the natives say, of a dragon who swam in there centuries ago and can't find its way out.

Less than 20 miles, but hundreds of years, away is the tiny island of Niihau. According to legend, no one may ever visit there, and if a Hawaiian leaves, it's forbidden to return. It's not quite true. Visitors are allowed to go to Niihau, but only invited guests. And Hawaiians who leave are welcomed back. But not many ever leave because they like it there.

A century ago, Elizabeth Sinclair, a Scottish woman from New Zealand, having lost her husband, packed all her belongings and her children and grandchildren into a small boat and set out for Canada. She stopped off in Honolulu where she met King Kamehameha IV. He was so charmed by her that he offered to give her some land nearby. She had cattle ranching on her mind, and so refused the offer and sailed on. She went to Vancouver, but didn't like what she found there, so she loaded up the schooner again and went back to Hawaii.

She paid the king $10,000 for the 72-square mile island of Niihau, and got some coastal land on Kauai in the bargain. Her son-in-law, a man named Robinson, became the lord of the island, and when he died about 30 years ago, his widow and five children became the sole owners of Niihau.

There are 300 people living there now, all pure-blooded Hawaiians, all speaking the pure, unadulterated language of their forefathers. There are public schools, and the children are taught English. But none of them takes it too seriously. There aren't any dogs, policemen or even movies on Niihau. During World War II, when, incidentally, they had an uninvited guest in the form of a Japanese pilot who crash-landed there, radios were introduced by the U.S. Army Signal Corps. Today, all the people who live there are crazy about radios. And recently the government, with the kind of wisdom governments everywhere are so fond of showing, has sent them battery-powered TV sets.

For years, the islanders earned their living by raising cattle and sheep and keeping bees. The cost of transporting cattle off the island to the marketplace has put them out of that business. And the low prices paid for wool took all the profit out of raising sheep. Today they earn their keep by making grass mats, leis and other handicrafts for sale in

Honolulu.

In spite of the intrusion of TV sets and newspapers and other trappings of the 20th century, Niihau is one of the last places on earth where simple feudal life still exists. It's the only place where old Hawaii still lives.

There are other islands in Hawaii that tourists never see. Kahoolawe is used for target practice by the U.S. military, and visiting there would surely be dangerous to your health. Lehua and Molokini as well as Kuala are all barren rocks sitting there like the Ancient Mariner, surrounded by water without a drop to drink.

There are many barren spots in this paradise they call Hawaii. In fact, with 49 other states to choose from, NASA picked Hawaii as the place best suited to give the Apollo astronauts a good idea what they'd find when they went to the moon. It's not all dry, of course. The wettest spot in the world is a mountaintop in Kauai that gets an average of 40 *feet* of rain a year. In 1948, they got 624.1 inches of rain up there…a little more than 52 feet.

But Hawaii is mainly gentle breezes and bright sunshine, and that's why people go there. A lot of people go there to watch the sun *set* because it probably doesn't set as beautifully anywhere in the world as it does on the Kona Coast on the big island that gave all the islands its name, Hawaii. The huge volcano Mauna Loa keeps the wind away from the coast, and every morning it's bright and sunny there because the clouds can't get over the mountain. They often win the battle by the middle of the day, and when they do, they act like an umbrella that keeps the hot sun off the beach and the temperature down. Combined with the rich soil of the volcano, it makes a perfect atmosphere for growing coffee, and plenty of it is grown there. In fact, Hawaii is the only place in the United States where you'll find coffee plantations. Kamehameha I and his chiefs used the Kona Coast as their principal playground. The king spent his last years there, fishing for the fabulous game fish, including the Pacific blue marlin. But when they were all younger, they didn't think anything in the world was more fun than holua…tobogganing down the side of a snowless mountain. The remains of one of their runs is still there, a slide about a mile long on a hillside. They had it covered with grass cuttings and had themselves a ball!

One of the biggest cattle ranches in the United States is right near the Kona Coast. The Parker Ranch has been growing since a New Englander, John Palmer Parker gave up the life of a sailor to become a cowboy in 1847. His spread was no threat to the big guys who were getting established in the American Southwest at the time. It was only two acres. It's grown today to well over a quarter of a million acres. And it has the big advantage over its Texas competitors of that wonderful Hawaiian seacoast. And those sunsets!

Most of the beaches on the islands are made of fine white sand that feels terrific underfoot. It feels so good, in fact, that the missionaries, persuasive as they were, were never able to talk the Hawaiian people into wearing shoes. Even today, the islands aren't exactly a paradise for shoe salesmen. On the big island of Hawaii, that fine white sand comes in a variety of colors, including green at one point. But the most unusual is on the southern coast where the beaches and sand dunes are black.

This coast is the traditional home of the fire goddess Pele, and the black sand is just one example of her work. Another is the island itself, which is more than twice as big as all the other islands put together. And it's getting bigger because Pele is still at it. She breathes fire through the huge Mauna Loa volcano, and sometimes, when the mood strikes her, she makes Kilauea boil over. The territory around the mountains, now a national park, is an experience no one ever forgets. The black beaches and sand dunes, made of pulverized lava, are just the beginning. Going into Hawaii Volcanoes National Park is like going into another world. Thousands of acres are covered with cinders and a hard crust of lava that has been hardened into patterns that look like a pan of molasses that's been neglected. There's a whole forest of the ghosts of trees whose roots were sealed off by a lava flow; and another living forest that was left undisturbed when a lava river forked around a 100-acre space to form a green island in the midst of the desolation. There's a hotel and a golf course in the park, in probably the most unusual setting for either one anywhere in the world.

But what makes the park truly unique is Mauna Loa and Kilauea, both very much alive. It's possible to get to the top of Mauna Loa and look into its awesome fire pit. But getting there isn't half the fun. There's a paved road about halfway up the side of the mountain, but after that, it's an 18-mile hike to the summit. Hardy hikers say the trip is worth it, but most people prefer to take their word for it. And after all, there's another volcano right next door, and it's spectacular too.

Kilauea also has the advantage of being easier to climb. The trip to the top is 9,000 feet shorter, and with a little bit of luck, people who take the trip see volcanic activity inside the crater, even an occasional eruption. Every once in a while, somebody reports seeing Pele herself. She's beautiful and still young, they say, with long flowing red hair. Sometimes she even talks to them to explain where the next river of fiery lava will go. When that happens, there's no guarantee it will actually happen that way, though. Pele has been known to change her mind.

Most people drive around the rim in their cars. There is an observation platform on the brink of it, giving an unforgettable view of the fire pit inside. The pit is like a big kettle about a half-mile around and about 750 feet deep. That's where the spectacular fire fountains and melted lava come from. Most of the time, the lava stays inside the crater, but now and then, Pele decides to put on a show and the whole thing spills over. When it does, the island grows a little more.

Every now and then, nature takes a little away from the big island. Huge tidal waves, which the natives call *tsunamis*, have come roaring across the Pacific, even in recent times, to bring havoc to the island's main city, Hilo. Every time one has hit, Hilo has hit back, moving a little bit farther inland and putting up bigger and better breakwaters against the

...ext tsunami.

They're a tough bunch, these Hawaiians. Nothing keeps ...em down for long. They endure volcanoes, tidal waves, ...urist invasions, even missionaries, with good-humored ...arm. They'll jump at any excuse for a good party, and the ...st idea for a party in any of the 50 states is an authentic ...awaiian luau.

Today luaus are staple fare at most of the big hotels, and ...u'll find everybody from the Hauloowoona chapter of ...adassah to the friendly sons of Polynesia sponsoring them ...r profit as well as for fun. In the beginning, the luau was ...e big event in small villages, a tradition similar to New ...ngland clambakes. The name itself means "taro leaf," which ...e old-timers used for food. Their parties were held in the ...nter of the villages, and everybody in town was ...vited...indeed, everybody in town helped prepare it. The ...tting, lit by festive torches, included the dazzling flowers ...d tropical foliage that sets the scene for so much of the ...arm of the islands.

It took the whole day to get a good luau together. First ...e men dug a huge pit and lined it with rocks. Then they ...ilt a fire to heat the rocks. Next, they split a pig open, ...led it with heated rocks and wrapped it in taro leaves. The ...g was buried in the pit and left to roast most of the day. By ...e time it was ready to eat, it was the best-tasting roast pork ...y culture ever devised.

But man cannot live by pork alone. Not at a luau. The ...ll of fare included roast chicken, laulau, a piece of pork ...rapped together with salmon and roasted, baked yams ...ith pineapple, shredded salmon mixed with fresh tomatoes ...d onions and eaten raw, and steamed taro leaves. Poi was ...cluded, too, served with dried seaweed. And for desert, ...conut cream pudding, called noupio.

When there was nothing special to celebrate, the average ...awaiian lived on poi, the mainstay of the diet in the islands ...r longer than anyone can remember. Mark Twain ...escribed it as something that looks like "...common flour ...ste, kept in large bowls formed of a species of guord and ...pable of holding from one to three or four gallons. Poi is ...epared from the taro plant...when boiled, it answers as a ...ssable substitute for bread. The buck Kanakas bake it

underground, then mash it with a heavy lava pestle, mix water with it until it becomes a paste, set it aside and let it ferment, and then it is poi – and an unseductive mixture it is, almost tasteless before it ferments and too sour for a luxury afterward. But nothing is more nutritious. When solely used, however, it produces acrid humors, a fact which sufficiently accounts for the humorous character of the Kanakas. I think there must be as much of a knack in handling poi as there is in eating with chopsticks. The forefinger is thrust into the mess and stirred quickly round several times and drawn as quickly out, thickly coated, just as if it were poulticed; the head is thrown back, the finger inserted in the mouth, and the delicacy stripped off and swallowed – the eye closing gently, meanwhile, in a languid sort of ecstasy. Many a different finger goes into the same bowl and many a different kind of dirt and shade and quality of flavor is added to the virtues of its contents."

If Mark Twain was implying that eating native food in Hawaii is bad for your health, don't believe it! Hawaiians are the healthiest people in the United States. Life expectancy in the U.S. is just under 73 years at this point. The average Hawaiian can expect to live almost 76 years. Hawaiian women, with the longest life span of any American, average almost 78 years. Hawaiian women almost never die in childbirth, and heart disease, cancer and stroke kill far fewer in Hawaii than anywhere else in the country. Of course, with that climate, they don't get pneumonia or flu very often, either. And to top it all off, the ratio of doctors to the population is among America's highest, even though there isn't much for any of them to do, apparently.

It isn't clear whether the "Aloha Spirit" keeps them alive or whether they stay around longer to enjoy the "Aloha Spirit." But that spirit is something that makes Hawaii unique among the 50 states.

It's a combination of remembering history and respecting tradition. It's taking joy from beauty and honoring grace. It's taking paradise seriously.

Hawaiians do all those things. Their life is generally joyful, and joy is like a contagious disease...as anyone who has ever been close to it knows very well.

The waters around the islands of Hawaii provide some of the finest surfing anywhere in the world. Huge waves present not only a challenge for the most experienced surfers, but also opportunities for exciting photographs such as these at Waikiki, left and Kaimu.

Fine beaches are commonplace in Hawaii. Vacationers take advantage of the fine faciliti[es] afforded by Honolulu above, right and belo[w] *and Waikiki* center left.

Waikiki is featured top left *with one of Haw[aii's] most famous landmarks, Diamond Head, in t[he] background, and* bottom left *is shown Ala W[aikiki] harbor.*

Pictured at sunset overleaf *is Ala Moana Pa[rk,] favorite recreation spot.*

...ked by a considerable number of hotels, ...kiki Beach *above and above right is a* ...rite resort with sun-seekers and surfers *below* ...right. *A panorama of Ala Wai harbor is* ...*vn left.*

modern city of Honolulu, the capital of
aii, is shown left with, in the background, the
mark of Diamond Head. The new Capitol
ling below was completed in 1969.

aii Building above provides a vivid contrast
the past, epitomized top right, by the Island's
rame house, one of the restored architectural
ures in the Civic Center.

's Alley, Waikiki right, is situated on
uani Avenue and features several levels of
s, the whole designed in turn-of-the-century
as a reminder of the Honolulu of the days of
onarchs.

ding storm-clouds gather behind the
rapers lining Ala Wai harbor left, and palm
front Honolulu harbor right.

imposing statue below represents
ehameha the Great, Conqueror of the Islands.

red on these pages is the Kodak Hawaii
Show, which takes place at the Waikiki Shell
hu. The colorful costumes create an exotic
phere that typifies most people's idea of
ii.

ula was originally a religious dance,
med before the rulers or the people, in honor
e specific occasion or to propitiate the gods.
nowadays usually tell a story or describe a
n through the picturesque medium of
s movement. In the early part of the 19th
y, New England missionaries, shocked by the
lity of the hula, compelled the native women
r long dresses – holokus – and the resulting
visual sensuality was then balanced by even
xaggerated body movements. Today the hula
ormed principally for tourists and their
as, but this at least ensures the continuance of
nating and historic spectacle.

...vy skies add drama to the photograph
...vious page of the Koolau Range taken
... Laie Point.

... Polynesian Cultural Center all pictures
..., lies just outside Laie, on the windward
... of the island of Oahu. The center
...sents the whole span of Polynesia and its
... in one area, and it contains replicas of
...ages of old Hawaii, Tonga, Tahiti,
...noa, Fiji and the New Zealand of the
...oris. Visitors may walk around the
...er, take a guilded tour in an outrigger
...oe, or on an open tram. Canoe pageants are
... twice daily in the lagoon, along the
...ks of which the villages are situated.
...re are demonstrations of various
...ynesian crafts, entertainment in the form
... inging and dancing, and explanatory
..., at each village, on various aspects of
... different cultures

...ch of Honolulu's nightlife draws on
...dition, updated to provide 20th century
...ertainment such as that provided at the
...lies Polynesia this page.

... un sets behind the palm trees of Waikiki
...e.

... shoots high into the air from the Halona
...-hole, above left *a hole in the roof of a*
...erged lava tube, near Koko Head, formed
...g the last of Oahu's eruptions.

...s below *and* below left *were pictured at*
...analo Bay. *Apart from sandy bays such as*
...much of the Waimanalo coast is protected by
...f fortress-like proportions.

...a Beach top right, *near Kaena Point, was*
...s the setting for 19th century Lahaina in the
...wood film 'Hawaii'.

...orth shore of Oahu features huge winter surf,
...ularly along the stretch of coast from Kawela
...imea Bay center right, *where some of the*
...s reach a frightening height of thirty feet.

...om right *is shown Makapuu Beach Park,*
... is famous for its facilities for body surfing.
...ore lies Manana (Rabbit) Island, so named
...se it supports a small colony of European
... brought by a sugar planter towards the end of
...st century.

*l beauty and the outdoor life of the Islands is
red on these pages while overleaf are shown
win tunnels cut through the Koolau Range,
Kailua Bay in the background.*

Parrots preen and display their brilliant pluma[ge] in Paradise Park right.

The elaborate and highly decorative weather va[ne] above is at the Kahuku Sugar Mill, which was operational from 1890 to 1972.

A popular breakfast fruit in many countries is papaya, seen growing below.

Small boats swing at anchor top left in Kaneo[he] Bay.

The main feature of the Valley of the Temples, [a] memorial park in Ahuimanu Valley, is Byodo-[In] Temple center left, a replica of the famous tem[ple] of the same name in Kyoto, Japan. It contrasts strongly with the Mormon Temple bottom lef[t] near Laie.

The rocky coastline below is at Kalanianaole, [and] the sacred carp overleaf were photographed at [the] Byodo-In Temple.

...w the grandeur of the soaring cliffs of Kauai ...nd stands the lighthouse at Kilauea Point left.

...ee churches are featured on this page: above, ...nd the Royal Poinciana Tree, is the Lutheran ...rch of the Nations, right is the United ...hodist Church at Kaumakani and below is ...a Church, Koloa.

...erleaf is shown the magnificent Fern Grotto ...r Wailua.

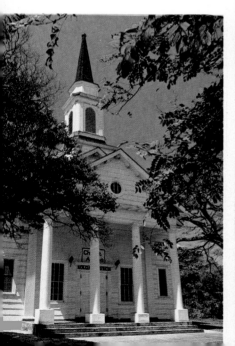

Tourism and sugar vie for the position of Kau[ai's]
leading income producers. Top left are the
McBryde Sugar Company's cane fields, back[ed by]
the Lihue Mountains, and below are the ca[ne]
fields near Lihue. Sugar cane harvesting is sh[own]
above near Kaumakani.

The flooded salt ponds center left are near
Hanapepe.

Lush vegetation and cactus below share the
fertile land in Hanapepe Valley bottom lef[t.]

Cloud hanging on the peaks of the mountain[s is a]
feature of Kalalua Valley right.

Offshore currents make swimming hazardous
the waters off Lumahai Beach above left but
nevertheless, a very attractive and much-
photographed area.

The Lumahai River is shown above as it mak
way to the open sea.

The beautiful scene left was photographed at
Polihale State Park, a 140-acre reserve at the s
end of Na Pali.

Poipu Beach below right provides shallow co
for children as well as smooth water for swimm
and surf suitable for boards. Nearby is Brenne
Beach, which is ideal for body surfing.

Above Makahuena Point below, the road en
the crater formed during Kanai's last eruptior

The peaceful scene above right was taken at
Barking Sands Beach.

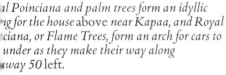

al Poinciana and palm trees form an idyllic
ng for the house above *near Kapaa, and Royal
ciana, or Flame Trees, form an arch for cars to
under as they make their way along
way 50* left.

*nd a foreground of colorful flowers, Wailua
r* below and center right *courses through the
ant greenery of the Wailua River State Park.*

*e upper reaches of the Wailua River are the
lua Falls* top right, *where the waters of the
plunge over a high canyon wall.*

magnificent Opaekaa Falls bottom right,
onsidered to be the most beautiful on Kauai.

*incredible greenery of the Hanalei Valley
leaf is bisected by the blue ribbon of the
alei River.*

By anyone's definition, the Na Pali coast abov*
left and right *can only be described as spectac*
Huge cliffs rise 2,000 to 3,000 feet from the se
and great folds and ridges form deep valleys th
reach far inland.

The geyserlike spray of Spouting Horn below*
accompanied by a moaning sound said to be th
sorrowing cry of a legendary lizard which has
trapped for forgotten ages in the lava tube bel

Some of Hawaii's finest gardens are to be found *Kauai*. One such is *Menehune Garden at Nawiliwili* top left and below, *in which the central feature is a giant weeping banyan tree, huge aerial roots of which grow into the ground forming new trunks* bottom left.

A common and attractive mode of transport in Hawaii is the outrigger canoe above.

The horses center left *were photographed high the Hanalei Mountains.*

The evening sun picks out the texture of almos defoliated trees in Waimea Canyon above rig *and the Royal Poinciana Tree* below right *proudly displays its flame-colored flowers, which justly earn for it the name 'Flame Tree'.*

Heavy skies add a sense of timelessness and a brooding, almost menacing air to the Pali coast, Molokai top left, one of the most spectacular coastlines in Hawaii.

Waves crash onto the beach in the shelter of Halawa Bay center left.

The island of Molokai, the 'Friendly Isle', is well-known for its leper colony and the splendid work that has been done there to help sufferers of this disease. Above is pictured the house of J. Brede, a guide at the colony, and the grave below right is that of Mother Marianne, who was one of the colony's leading helpers.

The red-roofed church of Our Lady of Sorrows above right is set among palm trees near Kalauaha.

Strange rock outcrops are shown bottom left on the sands at Kepuhi Bay Beach. In the distance is the Sheraton Resort at Kepuhi Park, where the golf course above is located.

Near Kaunakakai stands the Kapuaiwa coconut grove below which was planted over one hundred years ago by Kamehameha V.

Modern Hawaiian history began at
Lahaina, on the island of Mauii.
Kamehameha the Great established
residence here after his conquest of M
and some of the first missionaries from
Boston landed here in 1823.

A catch of Marlin is shown being lande
Lahaina Harbor top left, which is also
shown left and right. The train and eng
above and below have been rebuilt to
authentic 1890-1910 specifications. Or
to haul sugar cane, they now carry tou
along six miles of track on a journey ba
the days of Victorian Hawaii.

The huge bulk of Kahakuloa Head *top left* rises almost vertically from the sea at its base.

Picturesque Hana Highway winds its way around the coast *center left*, dropping down now and again to isolated little bays and coves.

At Kihea *above* there were once plans for a multi-million dollar resort. The extent of project was later reduced but Kihea remain the major growth district in the state.

The natural arch formation *bottom left* is the Waianapanapa State Park, which contains Waianapanapa Cave where, so legend says, a Hawaiian princess was murdered by her jealous husband, and her sighs and sobbing still echo in the cave.

Palm trees reach down to the water's edge *below* on the surf-washed Keanae Penins

The Silversword – *Argyroxiphium sandwicense* – is a dramatic and unusual annual found growing only on the Islands. grows in volcanic ash and cinders and is shown *right* in the crater of Haleakala volcano, where it is warm in the daytime and very cold at night and the air is extremely dry.

s quite remarkable to think that the exotic
versword plant on page 89 can and does grow
such a seemingly inhospitable environment as
t in Haleakala crater above and below left.

nsets are a great feature of the Hawaiian
nds, typified by that at Kahului Bay above.

ow are the lovely Haipuaena Falls and right
ao Needle, a green-mantled peak in the Iao
ley State Park.

...ight be expected, because of their geographical ...ion and climate the Hawaiian Islands ...ort a great variety of beautiful and colorful ...

...delicate, dwarf poinciana above left is a ...cal genus of the Caesalpinia family which ...named after De Poinci, a French West Indian ...ernor.

...e are some 550 species of Anthurium below ...all of which are members of the Arum family.

...exotic and aptly-named bird of paradise ...r top right grows from rhizomes and reaches ...ght of three feet or more.

...e are many thousands of orchids grown ...lly for hybridization, of which the lovely ...r Vanda is a particularly fine example above.

...er right is the beautifully symmetrical ...a and below is the delicate and pretty ...an jasminium.

...vly-emerging flower of the glory bush is ...red in beautiful detail bottom right.

More of Hawaii's plentiful, and sometimes exo[...] plant life is shown on these pages.

Above is a deep red spray of bougainvillaea an[...] top left is another of the family of orchid hybr[...] this one known as the Cattleya.

A rocket protea is shown below, and center le[...] is a flower of the Kuhio vine, or Brazilian glor[...]

There are about 120 species of the heliconia, spread throughout tropical America and the western Pacific.

The specimen below is the giant red and yello[...] variety.

Water lilies bottom left are not, of course, confined to any one particular region, but the Hawaiian Islands provide ideal conditions for growth of very beautiful examples.

The unusual plant shown right is the ixora.

A lei is a garland of flowers worn around the n
It is usually given as a token of welcome or
farewell. Traditionally, on being presented wit
lei when leaving the Islands, the visitor should
it into the waters of the harbor as the ship depe
The lei drifting gently back to shore is taken as
indication that the traveller will also return,
someday, to the Islands. In Hawaii, Lei Day is
celebrated as a day of friendship on May 1st.
Plumeria above and all pictures left are basi
flowers used in the making of these charming
garlands.

The hibiscus below is the State Flower of the
State of Hawaii.

The rich green foliage and flowers above right
those of the Pentas and below right is a fine
example of the flowers of the candle bush.

...village of Kailua is one of the main hotel and ...areas on the island of Hawaii. Much of the ...ainment centers, not surprisingly, on the ...: There are boats to charter for cruising or ...g, larger pleasure craft cruises such as those ...d by Capt. Bean above and center right, ...acing canoes bottom right.

...d the aptly-named boat below left, stands ...aikaua Church and Hukihee Palace, which ...o featured overleaf.

Mauna Kea Beach Hotel below left *fronts*
...vely bay above left. *The hotel stands in*
...acres of tropical oasis. Inland are the Kohala
...ntains and there is also much of interest in the
...diate area, including a restored Hawaiian
...and the remnants of a heiau *or temple.*

...leet of cruisers above *is at anchor in*
...kohau Harbor, on the Kona coast.

...un and the sound of waves typify Kailua
.

...hou Bay below *was once a canoe landing*
...for Kona's fishermen.

...un sets overleaf *behind St. Peter's Catholic*
...ch.

...or Honolulu, Hilo, in Hawaii, has the ...port on the Islands as well as a particularly ...bor pictured on these pages, and the ...iliuokalani Gardens above.

海王東京丸
KAIWO MARU TOKYO

It would be difficult to imagine a more beauti[ful]
setting for a golf course than that above at M[auna]
Beach on the Kona coast.

Nestled among the palm trees is the tiny Cat[holic]
church of St. Peter's, Kahaluu left.

Akaka Falls below, in Akaka Falls State Pa[rk]
drop 420 feet, in contrast to the gentle-seemin[g]
cascade of 100 feet Hapuna Falls right.

Dense vegetation almost blots out the sunligh[t]
Ohia Tree Fern Forest overleaf.

...lhouettes of palm trees and the moon hanging ...ove the horizon lend an almost magical quality ... Kahaluu Beach left.

...ava rubble and palm trees are shown above at ...ilolii, a tiny Hawaiian-Filipino fishing ...mmunity at the south end of Kona on Hawaii.

...awaii's rugged, surf-pounded coast is shown on ...is page. Top right is Opihikao, near Kaimu; ...nter right is the Maulua Gulch waterfall on ...e Hilo coast; bottom right are the lava cliffs ...ar Kaimu and below, seen from Waipio Valley ...okout, is Waipio Bay.

...alf a mile of boardwalk on top of cinders and ...rough a skeleton forest along Devastation Trail ...erleaf, ends at Kilauea Iki Overlook and Puu ...ai, a huge cone of ash and pumice resulting from ...e eruption of Kilauea Iki in 1959.

Steam still rises menacingly from Halemauma Kilauea crater center left.

Black Sand Beach is shown top left and belov and bottom left is Puhaluu Village, on Black Sand Lagoon on the Kona coast.

Featured right is one of the fierce-looking statu guarding the City of Refuge far right.

The view above was taken from Kahaluu Bea and overleaf is a typical lava field on Hawaii's west coast.

The Parker Ranch this page is reputedly *largest private ranch in the U.S.A. It cover 200,000-acres and was started at the begir the 19th century by John Palmer Parker, a who decided to stay in Hawaii and worked Kamehameha the Great, rounding up catt had returned to the wild. From them he dev a domestic herd and acquired the land on u founded his ranch.*

Gaily painted churches are very much a fea the Hawaiian Islands. The two examples s here are at Kaimu above right *and St. Ber Catholic Church on the Kona coast below*